A

And Otl **ons of**

Self Defense

Pat Smith

Acknowledgements

This volume is the fruit of decades of experience studying and teaching self-defense and hand-to-hand combat. I owe all of my teachers a special word of thanks for opening my eyes to the variety of ordinary objects that can be transformed into self-defense weapons.

Although I have had many occasions to defend myself on the street, I have never had to rely upon improvised weapons in order to defend myself. I always have some tool on my person that could be used as a weapon for self-defense, but every time I was attacked on the street, whenever I had time to pull a weapon, I had time to escape, and that is what I did: escape.

The many times where I was unable to escape without physically defending myself using martial techniques, I had no time to pull a tool or weapon with which to defend myself; I was left to my bare hands . . . and feet, and elbows, and head, etc.

That being said, there are times where defensive tools can come in handy.

Some of the recommendations I share in this short book, I learned from my teachers. Most, however, are suggestions I have come up with on my own based on my own experience surveying my regular ordinary surroundings. I learned to do this from many of my own teachers. When I first began thinking about what objects in a room could be used in self-defense, it took quite a lot of effort and creativity on my part. After about a year of doing this, it became instinctual. Now, whenever I enter a room, walk down the street, enter a building, etc., I don't even have to think any more about what objects could become self-defense tools in a pinch—I automatically just see possibilities. My hope is that this little book will help you to do the same. Such a mentality will take practice and effort on your part, but it is worthwhile.

Contents

Introduction

In today's world, you can be attacked wherever you find yourself. Most martial arts schools persist in training students for classical attacks, attacks which are unlikely to happen in today's world. Such classical attack scenarios have their place within martial arts, but to stay safe in today's world, you need to learn how to improvise based on your ordinary surroundings.

Everyone knows that the presence of a weapon for defense can increase your chances of survival. There are at least three difficulties with carrying weapons of defense on your person:

(1) Weapons, like guns, defensive knives, etc., take training to use properly. Without such training you run the very serious risk of misusing the weapon, doing serious (perhaps fatal) harm to yourself or to innocent bystanders, and having the weapon taken from you and used against you or against others.

(2) Such weapons are not able to be carried (safely, legally, or practically) everywhere you might find yourself. Legally speaking, if you are outside of your house, few states or countries allow you to carry just any weapon. Moreover, if you're on an airplane, you're even more limited. If you're in a pool or in the ocean at the beach, practically speaking your even more limited.

(3) In real life self-defense situations, you rarely have time to pull a weapon from your holster, pocket, shirt, boot, or from wherever you might be keeping it. There's often just not sufficient time. If you get attacked at a restaurant, bar, bookstore, or coffee shop, unless you have your gun or knife in hand, you might be out of luck.

What I hope to do in this book is teach you to be more aware of your surroundings—not just for the purposes of keeping safe and avoiding danger—but, for the purpose of instantly assessing what tools you have around you in your natural setting that could become effective self-defense instruments if that immediate need should arise.

If the only thing that happens as a result of your reading this book is that you begin the habit of looking around you for potential weapons of self-defense, then this book will have been a success. We're going to cover a lot of different sorts of improvised weapons, objects that you probably wouldn't think of as weapons. This will be things on hand that you don't have to worry about hiding because no one will consider them to be weapons; in fact they're not. These objects will never be the "best" for combat. But what good is having the "best" with you but effectively unavailable?

The objects I cover in this book are readily available in our ordinary lives. I'm not recommending that you start practicing using the following objects as weapons. What I hope to do is spark your imagination so that you can think of other objects, not listed in this book, that you find in your ordinary day-to-day activities.

In the course of this book, I will not only cover potential weapons, but also how to use them, and what target areas to go for. I know this seems to violate my usual principle of not "teaching" via books, but in this case, these are not strictly speaking complicated martial arts techniques. Rather, these are the sorts of general defensive moves anyone can use.

Always bear in mind, the best "weapon" in any of these situations, will be a means of escape. With that in mind, you should always have in mind a potential escape exit. There are two areas from ordinary life that should help us think about the importance of escape exits. The first is flight. Before travelling anywhere by plane, the airlines ask us to look around and locate the nearest exit. Why? They tell us why: in case of an emergency. The same happens at the movie theater. Well, we should be doing the same all the time . . . in the case of an emergency.

So, take up this book and allow your imagination to expand. The result will be that you will become safer in the environments you inhabit. The knowledge that you are safer will lead to your increased confidence, which will in turn make you less of a target to would be attackers. So my hope is that your reading this book will make the world a safer place for you, the reader. And, if an attack ever should come, you will be more prepared with the weapons you have on hand, wherever you are.

With that in mind, it's time to take a look at some of these improvised weapons of self-defense, beginning with a cup of coffee . . . .

Ch. 1: A Cup of Coffee

Yes, a cup of coffee can be an effective improvised weapon of self-defense, as the title of this book indicates. Not only can the hot liquid be used to scald an attacker's face, allowing you the moment you need to escape, but even if your coffee has cooled, when thrown in someone's face or eyes, can be used to force the attacker's natural reflexes to jump into action. When the attacker blinks and is momentarily disoriented, you have your opportunity to break free and run. Moreover, the cup itself, if it is hard plastic, porcelain, or something similar— as opposed to paper or plastic throw away ones for on-the-go—the cup can be used as a blunt striking object.

In this chapter, we'll bring up several different ordinary objects relating to beverages like coffee that can be used to defend yourself in a pinch. Most of these improvised weapons are one-shot deals; that is, they are not intended to be used for a prolonged fight, but rather are intended to be a rapid means of distracting the attacker (perhaps causing injury as well) so that you can get away to safety.

1.1: A Drink

Any liquid can be used to distract an opponent. If this liquid is ice cold, the momentary numbing pain from the cold liquid can greatly add to the distraction. If the liquid is super-hot, the damage inflicted might be severe. Some restaurants serve coffee so hot that it can cause severe burns. You would only want to use such steaming hot liquid as a weapon if you fear severe bodily harm.

Apart from the potential damaging effects of very cold or very hot liquid, the general distracting effect of liquid being thrown in your face or eyes is sufficient for this to be an effective if under-recognized improvised tool of defense. An opponent intent on attacking you will likely have to take a moment to wipe off their face after being splashed. This could afford you the opportunity to get away, or perhaps first push them out of the way or land another strike to aid your escape. A skilled martial artist can use the opportunity to put the attacker in a submission hold and await the police.

The most common liquids we come across on a regular basis are our drinks. Some readers might have chemicals and more dangerous liquids on hand on account of their unique jobs, but all of us have drinks on hand several times a day. So, always remember, whatever you're drinking can be used in a pinch as a self-defense tool to distract (or potentially injure) a would-be attacker.

1.2: Drinking Mugs

     As I already mentioned at the outset of this chapter, a coffee or tea mug can be an incredibly effective blunt object used for self-defense. You might only have one shot with the easily breakable porcelain mug. A sturdier mug, however, might withstand an entire attack where you can't flee. So how might this work?

Ordinarily you don't want to throw the mug. Unless you have many on hand, you automatically lose your weapon (or hand it over to the attacker) by throwing it. More than likely you'll miss entirely, and have just wasted an opportunity (and perhaps a good mug) with the careless throw. Just think about the spear. In the movies, spears are often thrown in war time.

Certainly spears have been and could be used in that way. In the martial arts, however, where a spear is an actual weapon that one can study (I've studied northern Chinese spear forms and techniques, for example), you rarely throw the spear. You only get one spear, and if you throw it, you've lost it (unless by chance your spear kills the opponent. In most of these forms, the techniques are like those of a staff, but with a sharp spear point at one end. There are a lot of stabbing and thrusting techniques, but you don't ordinarily let go of the spear; you retain it as you would a long staff. The same is the case with a coffee mug.

The best way to use a mug effectively in a self-defense situation is by holding the mug upside down, hand around the mug with at least two fingers through any handle, and your thumb or index finger on the bottom (now top) of the mug, so that any contents in the mug would fall on the ground—if you haven't drained the mug already or thrown the contents into the attacker's face.

The most effective strikes will be in the downward direction, using gravity as your ally. You want to strike down. You can strike from the either side as well, but that will take more skill. The easiest and most effective striking will be downward. A skilled martial artist might be able to bring the mug down effectively on an opponent's hands, or collar bone (which breaks fairly easily), but in general, you'll want to strike down on the fact . . . any part will do. The nose, the jaw, the cheek bone, below the eyes, the mouth. Any of these will be effective targets. The ear could be a good target as well.

I would avoid he forehead, because it's the hardest part of the human body and most likely to break your porcelain mug, and hurt your own hand as well from the shock of the impact, although the blood you may draw from the opponent's forehead might temporarily blind them, since head wounds (even minor ones) tend to bleed a lot. In an emergency, don't worry about target aiming, just strike down on the face. Used in such a way, an ordinary drinking mug can be a devastating blunt weapon.

1.3: Bottles

    If mugs can be effective improvised weapons of self-defense, then what about bottles? Bottles too can be just as effective, or even more so, depending on the bottle. A thin glass beer or soda bottle might only last one hit before breaking, but a thicker wine, beer, or soda bottle might last several strikes and function like a small club. Of course, if your bottle breaks, it can then be used as a sharp weapon. You have to be careful with broken bottles, though, because they're easy to get cut with. You might injure yourself as much or more with that broken bottle than your attacker.

In general, bottles can be effective clubs. If you are carrying a full thick plastic water bottle, as seem so popular these days, that can be an effective clubbing instrument. The main targets could be almost anywhere. Your most effective targets will remain the face and head. With the longer reach of a bottle (over a coffee mug), you'll be more effective at hitting the torso, the belly, ribs, etc. You can use it against hands, arms, legs. Smash up into an attacker's groin, etc. An unexpected hit to the face or head from a hard bottle can be more effective than throwing liquid in an attacker's face, and might even knock them unconscious, depending on how hard a hit you give them.

A skilled martial artist could use a hard glass coke bottle, or wine bottle, to kill an attacker. An untrained defender, however, might still kill someone by accident, especially with a hit to the head with a hard bottle. You do have to be careful. One thing martial artists learn after only a few years of training, is how easy it actually is to take someone's life—at least physically speaking. Psychologically killing can be far more difficult. The point I'm making is that you have to be careful. The more skilled you are the easier it is to defend yourself and get out of a dangerous situation with doing minimal damage to the attacker. That often takes real skill. With less skill more damage is often necessary, and certainly more difficult to avoid.

If the bottle breaks and you use it as a cutting weapon, there are a number of things to keep in mind. First of all, you've changed the nature of the weapon. It's no longer a blunt object, but a cutting one. One of the most frightening aspects about sharp weapons is that they don't need power to be effective. If you merely touch someone with a sharp piece of glass, a sharp knife, or a sharp sword, you can cut them. Equally frightening, especially with very sharp weapons, is that you might not even know you've been cut.

Another point about sharp weapons should be brought up at this point. There are lots of "knife fighting" manuals and videos out there. Knives are often advertised (I chose that word carefully) as choice weapons of self-defense. They are advertised as such especially be knife-manufacturers, and others who are making money off of them. And the truth is that a knife can be an effective tool in the right hands during an attack.

You must keep in mind, however, that any sharp object used in a physical conflict is fundamentally a killing weapon. That doesn't mean that it will always kill. But a skilled martial artist would never pull a knife out unless the situation warranted the death of the opponent. This is one difference between a knife and a staff.

A police officer might use a club or staff to defend herself or to subdue an attacker. A police officer would be foolish, however, to pull out either a knife or a gun in violent situation that did not warrant use of lethal force—a nice term for killing someone. That doesn't mean a police officer should kill someone every time they pull out a knife or a gun. It simply means you shouldn't pull out a lethal weapon like that if the attacker's death is not warranted at that point.

A staff or club, on the other hand, can be just as lethal in the hands of a skilled practitioner, but you have so many more options. You would have to be very desperate, and somewhat skilled, to use either a gun or a knife as a blunt object (while minimizing the chance of it cutting or shooting). Staffs and clubs are by definition blunt objects. They can kill when struck in the right targets with the right amount of force. They can also be used to disarm, subdue, etc.

If your bottle breaks and you decide to use the sharpened class to cut your attacker, you better be in a life-or-death situation, or you'll have to face the consequences, including legal consequences. Now, if you're in danger of death, going to jail where you will likely be physically and sexually assaulted (violently in both cases) might seem preferable. You have to do what you have to do to survive. In such a case, you want to stab, not slash, with the broken bottle. Your target should probably be the face. You might blind them in the eyes, you might cut their neck and throat, resulting (eventually) in their death, but you'll definitely carve them up for the police to track down (and drench them in blood) with a strike to the face.

Why not slash? Less jarring. You want to stop your opponent from killing you, or at least create a means of your escape. Slashing will certainly do damage to them, and might kill them if it's in the throat or neck area, but it takes time for people to bleed to death. This is one of those things that frustrates me to no end about knife defense advertisements. They make it seem that if you have "this" knife—simply purchase it and carry it on your person—and you'll emerge from any conflict and live to tell the tale.

Bullshit. If you carry a knife, most of you will be more likely to use it, with the overconfidence (i.e., false confidence, false sense of security) you have, convinced by the advertisement or the sexiness of the blade, etc. You'll be less likely to look for an escape, and more likely to want to show you blade (which is never meant to be shown, and only meant to be used effectively and hidden). Moreover, these advertisements—and many of the so-called knife experts out there (who have never been attacked by a knife wielding opponent, and never seen an actual knife fight up close and personal)—show their utter ignorance. They just want to make a buck and it doesn't matter if it's at the expense of your life. They're legally covered by their disclaimers.

Let's be honest. As someone who has been attacked by knife-wielding assailants (and I'm fortunate to still be alive), and as someone who has witnessed bloody knife fights, I can tell you what these are like. The first thing is scary as shit. I would much rather have someone put a gun in my face than a knife . . . and I've had both. Whenever a student asks me what the best defense is if someone pulls a gun (or knife) on you and they ask for your walled, I always respond, "Hand over your wallet." That's the best defense. It's different if they're slashing away at you, or trying to physically harm you or someone you love. But if they're just after your money, give it to them. It's not worth it.

Many of my martial arts instructors have been attacked with knives. Two of them were mugged (attempted at least), and they both emerged (not unscathed, but they survived, and fared better than the wood-be muggers). Their approach would not be my approach, however. I would hand over my money. I could easily slip on a banana peel. Anything could happen. When your life is at stake, your money is not worth your life.

The reason I am belaboring this point here is both so that I don't have to return to it in detail below when we discuss other sharp instruments, but also so that you live your life with eyes wide open. Seasoned "knife fighters" is a thing of the movies. It's not real. I know a number of skilled martial artists who have had to use a knife against a knife . . . on one or perhaps two occasions in fifty or more years ! ! ! !

I also knew "knife fighters" in gangs and on the street. NOT ONE of them is alive today. They are all dead. Some of them died in prison, but most in knife fights. Some bled to death, at least one died of an infection from a knife wound. The thing about a knife fight is that both parties have knives. Knives cut. You don't always feel cuts from sharp instruments. You can bleed to death from a cut (depending on where it is, how deep, how it is treated, etc.). Moreover, it takes time to bleed to death. Unless you behead your opponent (a popular method of ending the fight in traditional Filipino systems with their traditionally large knives—we'd probably call them swords—in the Philippines), they might deliver a fatal wound to you after you've delivered a fatal wound to them. A fatal throat cut doesn't end the fight instantly. The other person can still deliver more than one fatal cut to you before bleeding to death.

If you slash someone's throat with a broken bottle—even if it ends up killing them in the end—they still might kill you before they die. A thrust (stab), however, might jar them. You might not notice a slash at the moment. A stab, however, will be felt. A knife staff might feel like a hard punch. Imagine that to the face, only with a lot more blood. Be careful with broken bottles. They might cut you, they might kill your opponent, and you might survive the situation and land up in prison, ruining your life, the life of your colon, and many other things.

Ch. 2: A Dinner Plate

In the last chapter we explored various drinking instruments that you are likely to encounter throughout your day, and their potential to be transformed into an improvised weapon of self-defense. In this brief chapter, I want to spend a little time discussing the dinner plate—or dishes from any mealtime, for that matter.

You probably don't think of an ordinary plate as a useful tool of self-defense, but it actually can be quite effective in a self-defense situation. Again, as with coffee mugs, I wouldn't recommend throwing the plate, unless you were going to throw it as a distraction as you got another weapon (perhaps your hand gun from your hidden holster, or something else).

Plates can be an effective blocking instrument (against a knife or against a punch). They can also be used as a blunt object with which to strike an attacker's face, hands, head, etc. If your plate breaks, it might cut you or your opponent. A sharpened plate shard can be an effective cutting instrument, but see my cautions above on sharp objects.

How would you employ the plate most effectively? You could use the plate face (or bottom) as a shield against a knife. In any other scenario I would recommend striking (even for blocks against punches) with the plate edge. This is not simply because it will be less likely to break, but it will focus the power of the strike into a smaller hard surface area and thus be more devastating. The most effective targets will be the face, side of head, ear, hands, neck, and collarbone.

Even if you're using paper plates, however, so long as they are not wet and soaked through from food, they too can be transformed, with little effort, into a self-defense instrument. This one you should try at home. People are often amazed how effective a rolled up magazine or newspaper can be, but a paper plate is even more amazing, if less effective. If you roll up a paper plate, as you would a newspaper or magazine, so that it is a handheld kubotan like instrument, you should be able to get at least one good strike out of it.

Try rolling your paper plate (it won't work with Styrofoam) tightly into a small club. Hold it firmly in your hand (you might have to bend the rolled up plate in half) so that it is about the length of a long pen. Try one strike with it into a wooden table. Or try gently but firmly hitting yourself (be careful not to hurt yourself) on the hand or cheek. You don't want to use the lengthy part to strike but either end.

One strike to the face, to the throat, or to the eyes, might be enough to buy you time to escape. This is not the most effective instrument, but in an emergency it could potentially save your life, if it gives you a chance to escape.

Ch. 3: A Spoon and Other Eating Utensils

In this chapter we continue our discussion of the sort of ordinary objects you might find at the dinner table, or out and about with family or friends (or alone) at a restaurant, bar, coffee shop, or French cafe. We shall address the self-defense potential of ordinary eating utensils.

3.1: A Spoon

The spoon can be an excellent self-defense weapon. Either end of the spoon can be effective. It has cutting potential (although not lethal cutting potential in the way a knife might), cutting the face and head, but is also blunt. A sturdy spoon can be used like a kubotan for joint manipulation and pain compliance techniques. A spoon can also be used to stab. Unlike a stabbing knife that has a bottom for your thumb to grip the knife handle in a secure way, ordinary spoons have no such means of securing them for a sure stab. In the case of a spoon, you probably don't want to employ downward stabs, although you can. Instead, what might be more effective is to use your index finger and thumb to secure the spoon, either close to the spoon itself, or to the butt end. Then you can stab by jabbing. The face, eyes, throat, and top of hand, ribs, all become potentially useful targets. With more skill, a wooden or metal spoon can be used like a kubotan to manipulate joints, strike pressure points, etc.

A plastic spoon can easily be transformed into a (non-lethal) cutting instrument, particularly apt for superficially cutting the face, blinding the eyes, or cutting the head. All you do is snap off the plastic spoon, leaving the handle. The broken part of the handle, secured by index finger and thumb, becomes a cutting instrument (also useful for opening packages and envelopes.

3.2: A Fork

The fork functions very much like the spoon, with the exception that the point fork end is a better cutting instrument than a blunt spoon. It is especially good at cutting the forehead, eyebrows, cheek and face, as well as the hand, but is also effective at striking the eyes. I would think of a fork just like the spoon, except that the fork might get stuck in someone, as knives sometimes do, in which case you might have to slash it out.

3.3: A Butter Knife

     People don't usually associate dull butter knives with weapons of self-defense, and yet, butter knives can be exceptional blunt self-defense instruments. Certainly a butter knife won't cut someone the way a sharp knife will, although it can be a good stabbing weapon. An ordinary dull butter knife can become deadly when used to stab an attacker. A stab with a butter knife certainly can puncture the skin, especially in the abdomen, if the attacker is not too heavily layered. A stab to the throat can also prove deadly. Even a thrust with the back end, as with many other blunt objects, can rupture internal organs. So never underestimate the effectiveness of a dull butter knife in a self-defense situation.

At the same time, the butter knife can serve for joint manipulation, kubotan-like, techniques, just as can the spoon and the fork. The butter knife, however, can outperform either spoon or fork. This is due to the fact that the blade is dull and thus extends the kubotan-like capacity of this utensil. If the handle is sufficiently sturdy, you can grip the dull blade as a handle and use the actual handle as a blunt instrument like a mini club, to strike the opponent at vulnerable spots, either with the butt end, or the side of the handle itself.

3.4: A Steak Knife

    The steak knife's ability as a weapon of self-defense is obvious. It can be used like any other knife. Just bear in mind what has been said already about sharp instruments of self-defense. In the future, I will write more about utilizing knives in self-defense situations, and about defending oneself against knife-wielding

---

opponents. This seems to be a popular topic, but so many so-called "experts" are giving bad advice. In fact much of what I read on this topic I would consider to be deadly advice; it's liable to get the reader killed or have them wind up in jail. So I plan on venturing onto that topic to help set the record straight and cut through the myths and deceptive advertisements to help you stay as safe as possible.

For the moment, I'll limit myself to a few practical concerns. If you do choose to use a steak knife, or other sharp instrument that you have on hand, in a self-defense encounter, you must treat it like you would a gun. Neither are to be used to threaten or scare off your opponent. If you pull a gun or a knife in self-defense, you have to be ready to *kill* your opponent. Do not bother with a gun or a knife unless you are prepared to kill your attacker, and, I would urge you to consider now, before it comes to that situation, whether or not it would be worth jail time. Jail can ruin your life. I'm not only talking about the violent rape and assault that will likely do severe harm to your body and psyche. Think too about loss of job, loss of time with your family and friends. A manslaughter or murder conviction—which can happen even in self-defense scenarios—can ruin your life.

Now, is it preferable to death? Yes. But, you have to ask yourself if the situation you're in is deadly. Someone asking for your money, even at gunpoint, is not necessarily such a situation. If someone pulls a gun at me in a restaurant—where I might have a steak knife on hand—and wants my money, I'm going to give it to them.

Chances are, in that situation, they won't kill me; they just want my money. Moreover, there are likely witnesses and possibly video surveillance, in which case the chances of my getting my money back are fairly high. Even so, my life is worth more to me than whatever spare cash I have on hand (credit/debit cards can be cancelled quickly when the banks are alerted). Is it worth jail time? No chance.

Change the scenario. Home invasion. Two thugs break into your house when you're not there. Your sixteen year old daughter is home alone, listening to music in the kitchen. They came in to rape and kill. She may not know that, but when one violently grabs her from behind under her arms and the other starts to help out, and she grabs the steak knife nearby, she knows she's in mortal harm's way. She attacks, perhaps kills. Completely different scenario. Might she go to prison? Unfortunately, in this day-and-age where so many victims, especially of sexual assault, are treated as perpetrators or liars—she might. But the stakes were much higher.

Again, my aged mother using a steak knife to defend herself at a restaurant will do much better legally than I would. On the other hand, I would be far more likely to use it successfully in defense. So, all of these things should be thought of in advance, so that when it's time to act, you do what you have to do to survive. Much better to use the umbrella you came in with than the steak knife. You might not have that choice, so you'll have to choose wisely, but even more so, you'll have to choose fast.

3.5: Chopsticks

Chopsticks are probably not the first thing you'd think of as a weapon of self-defense at a restaurant when you are attacked. Chopsticks, however, can be quite effective. The cheap easily broken wooden ones at your local Chinese takeout will probably not serve you very well if you are attacked—although you might be able to get one good jab to the eyes before they break. The sturdier chopsticks made of metal, plastic, or some other more solid material, might serve you well.

Some of the traditional Chinese martial arts, like Pa Kua Chang, utilize weapons that are shaped very much like chopsticks. Examples include the lesser known weapons like the emei piercers (or emeici), or the judge's pens. I wrote about these briefly in my popular *Palm Stick Self-Defense Guide*.

If the chopsticks are sufficiently sturdy, they can be effective, not only striking eyes, but striking other pressure points, striking the neck or throat, between the ribs, or in kubotan-like joint manipulation techniques. Chopsticks will be less usable in a self-defense situation for someone without the requisite skills, but they can still be used effectively to jab at the face and eyes if the situation requires it and you don't have sufficient training.

Ch. 4: Spare Change

The very loose change you carry in your pocket can be helpful in a self-defense situation. In my experience, the Japanese martial art of Ninjutsu—yes the art of the Ninja made popular by Hollywood—which I've never studied, is the main martial art that discusses use of spare change. This is perhaps because Ninjutsu styles are among the few that still teach and practice the art of shuriken

---

(throwing stars or spikes). You won't kill anyone by throwing spare change at them—nor are you likely to kill someone by throwing shuriken at them.

Unless they were dipped in poison, shuriken were not typically used to kill. Rather, shuriken were used as weapons of distraction, enabling the thrower to escape or pull a more lethal weapon. Loose change can function similarly, albeit less painful. Throwing coins—one at a time or all at once—at an attacker, can give you that split second needed to get away. Just chuck that change right in their face. Sounds silly, but it really can work. Their instincts will set in and they will blink, cover their face, turn away, etc. You'll have to be able to part with the change, but it could help you get away to safety. Splashing liquid in their face, or throwing stones, marbles, etc., all can work as well.

A roll of quarters, like you might take to the bank, can function as a blunt instrument to smash into your opponent, but you probably won't have that on hand. Any loose change or pebbles from the ground can help. Sand from the beach thrown in their eyes, or dirt, etc., can likewise be a distraction that you need to employ to get out of there.

Ch. 5: Car Keys

In contrast to many of the other examples included in this book—which you rarely hear about in the context of self-defense—car keys are a common everyday object that you often hear about as a potential self-defense weapon. At least I often find this on other blogs and articles. I've even seen self-defense classes teach how to use keys if you're being attacked. The problem I usually encounter is that the instructors so often get it all wrong. In most of the discussions I've seen or read the so-called experts instruct people to insert the different keys between the fingers so you can punch out with a closed fist and either rake the persons face or strike the face, neck, eyes, etc.

Try it on cardboard. Sure, you're likely to cut the cardboard, but you're also likely to find that the keys pushed back into your hand so that they're not as fully extended as when you began the strike. Try it on a tree...but carefully. If you strike too hard, you might hurt your hand, or even cut your fingers with the keys.

The best way to use a key (or keys) for self-defense is to select only one key and hold the key firmly between your thumb and index finger, the way you would when you're going to open a door. You might want to enhance the grip a bit by making sure the back of the key is securely snug against your hand. This is how you might normally hold a key, and it is much more effective. It will have a greater impact on the attacker and will be less likely to harm you in the process, although it still might hurt your hand if

you strike a hard surface like their head or
face.

Ch. 6: A Window Ice Scraper and Other Car Essentials

Chances are likely that you already carry in your car a number of ordinary tools that can be used as instruments of self-defense. Everything from a window scraper used to get ice off a windshield during the winter, to a flashlight, can be effective tools of self-defense in a pinch. You have to expand your imagination. Next time you get in your car, do a quick inspection to see what items you might have that could be employed as useful objects for self-protection. You might be surprised.

6.1: A Window Scraper

Your ordinary window scraper for icy days can be an effective tool of self-defense. Whether it is a long scraper, for mini-vans or full size vans, or a small handheld scraper you might pick up at a drug store, this can be used as a blunt staff-like object in an attack. Most sizes can be used to block strikes (or knife attacks), as well as to strike the face, head, arm, etc.

6.2: A Flashlight

My *Palm Stick Self-Defense Guide* includes a discussion of using flashlights as kubotan-like instruments. Flashlights can be incredibly effective. Unlike the small kubotan-like flashlights I recommended in that volume, however, for your car you should have a large flashlight, like MagLite's large C Cell Size 3, or something even larger. These heavy duty flashlights can serve like a short staff or club. You probably can't walk around the street with one of these hefty lights, but you certainly can keep one in your car within arm's reach.

6.3: A Tire Gauge

The small gauge you use to check your tire pressure can be used like a kubotan. You should always carry one of these in your glove compartment. You can even clip some of them to your keychain. If a kubotan draws attention attached to your keys, a tire air pressure gauge will no. These are excellent substitutes for kubotans and other palm sticks.

6.4: A Crowbar

The crowbar is a powerful option for a short staff in a pinch. This helpful tool can be turned into a quite deadly weapon instantly. One hit with a crowbar can spell the end of a violent encounter. They are helpful to have in your car in case of an emergency, and can be put to so many ordinary uses. If attacked, they can provide the distance and devastating power needed to escape alive. An excellent blocking tool, it becomes a truly devastating weapon when it comes to blows.

Ch. 7: An Office Pen and Related Office Tools

For those of you who work in an office setting, you are surrounded by potential weapons at all times. The office supply closet is a veritable weapons supply closet. You only have to look around you and expand your imagination. In this chapter we'll take a brief look at some of the ordinary objects you find around the office which can be transformed instantly into self-defense weapons.

7.1: A Pen

 As I explained in my *Palm Stick Self-Defense Guide*, a sturdy metal pen can easily be employed as a kubotan or palm stick. Some that are more pointy can be used to stab, but any solid and sturdy metal pen can be used to attack pressure points or for joint manipulation techniques. Even a cheap plastic pen can be used for one powerful strike at least. I am never without a solid metal pen, even at the beach. You can always use your pen to sign your name on a check, a bill, etc. They come in handy every day.

7.2: A Highlighter

   Believe it or not, a thick-bodied highlighter can be an effective palm stick. Like a kubotan, a thick plastic or metal highlighter can attack pressure points, assist in joint locks, etc. They can be devastating if used to strike the face with the bottom or top of the highlighter. If you prefer highlighters to pens, select a thick highlighter that suits your needs, and you'll never be without a legal kubotan.

7.3: A Pencil

The pencil, unlike the pen or highlighter, would not make a good kubotan...unless the pencil is a steel mechanical one. Pencils can, however, be effective stabbing instruments in an emergency. You can probably get at least one good stab in with a number 2 wooden pencil. These are the most popular shanks—make shift knifes—on the street. You probably never knew that. A stab wound from a pencil can be fatal without immediate medical attention.

7.4: Scissors

Although in skilled hands, a closed pair of sturdy metal scissors might be employed as a kubotan, the most obvious use of scissors in a self-defense situation is as a stabbing instrument. The back end of them (the handle) can also be employed effectively as a blunt weapon to stun the opponent.

7.5: A Stapler

The ordinary office stapler can be an effective blunt object, if it's of sufficient size. A large metal stapler can be used to hit the hands, face, or head. If you hit your opponent in the right place, you can knock him out with a solid strike from a stapler. You'd want to grip the stapler firmly by the stapling end, closing it as if you were going to staple some papers. You would then strike with the back end.

7.6: A Ruler

Depending on its size, you could use a ruler as a short stick with which to block an attack, and with which to deal out blows of your own. The thicker and larger the ruler the better. A Yardstick might be preferable, but whatever you have by your side (or desk) can be used. Even the flimsy foot long rulers some children still use at school, and provide at least a single solid strike before breaking.

7.7: Other Tools of a Trade

    If you don't work in a traditional office, but are instead fortunate enough to be surrounded by worker's tools (carpentry/construction/plumbing/electrician, etc.), then you have numerous potential weapons that can be used again-and-again, without breaking after an initial strike.

Examples abound. Hammers are perhaps the most effective. Some Filipino styles of martial arts even employ hammers in their martial arsenal. If I were a carpenter or construction worker, I'd carry a hammer with me at all times. Unfortunately I'm not so I would look rather odd walking around with a hammer at my side. Hammers and axes can be employed in similar ways, with different strengths and weaknesses. Axes are more effective for cutting and chopping (although hammers can do that too), and hammers are more effective for trapping and grappling (although axes can do that too).

Screwdrivers, especially flatheads, can be exceptional kubotans and stabbing instruments. You might be surprised how often a flat-headed screwdriver is used to stab someone. Emergency rooms across the country see victims of screwdriver wounds. Alright, this is certainly not as common as knife wounds, but they are more common than you might think. A large flathead screw driver can be used to block, strike like a small staff, attack pressure points, manipulate joints as in wrist locks, strike like a hammer with the butt end, and stab. A hard stab with a flat-headed screwdriver to the abdomen will pierce the belly. It's not a pretty sight, but might save your life in an emergency.

The list could go on and on for ordinary tools becoming unusual weapons at a moment's notice if you are attacked on the job. You have to use your imagination and see what you have around you on a daily basis.

Ch. 8: Trash Cans and Other Yard Equipment

Anyone who has a yard they have to maintain, also has ready weapons at their disposal if someone should attack while they are out and about. Home invasions have been on the rise for the last several decades, and increasingly they happen in broad daylight. If you happen to be outdoors and attacked, you very well may have a host of weapons around you.

8.1: Trash Cans

    So long as they are not too heavy, trash cans can be employed in your defense. The cans themselves can be placed between you and an attacker. If the cans are empty they can be thrown at the attacker. I would recommend keeping the lid if you throw the can, and don't throw the lid. The lid might be the most effective defensive part of the trash can. You can certainly use the lid to throw, but the lid would be more effectively employed as a shield to block attacks. This is especially the case if the attacker has a weapon other than a gun. A lid can protect you against a knife, stick, bat, ax, etc. It may not hold up equally well against all of these attacks, but it might give you a fighting chance. Moreover, if the lid is metal or solid, it can be used, like a shield, not only to block and defend against blows, but also to strike effectively at the opponent's head and face.

8.2: A Rake

The rake, or hoe, or similar long yard object, is an underappreciated weapon. A number of traditional Chinese martial arts actually have weapons that were rakes, e.g., the traditional 9 pointed rake. You must bear in mind that many of the weapons used in the martial arts, especially those used in Okinawan karate styles, originated as everyday objects, especially as farming tools. A rake or hoe can be used like a long staff, with the added metal component that can cut the attacker.

8.3: A Trowel

A small handheld trowel can be used as a cross between a small club and a knife in dealing with an attacker. Like a knife it can cut the face and head of an attacker, albeit less effectively. Like a small club, the trowel can be used to strike as a blunt object, albeit again less effectively.

8.4: A Shovel

     The shovel can also be used as an effective weapon of self-defense. The biggest drawback of the shovel, however, is it's weight. I would only use a shovel if the opponent was wielding a knife, and only then if I had no other long object at my disposal. As I've trained with staffs and spears of various sizes in the Chinese and Japanese martial arts, I would much prefer a rake or a hoe over a heavy shovel. But if it was the only long object I had at my disposal, and the attacker was wielding a knife, I wouldn't hesitate to use the shovel to disarm the attacker.

Ch. 9: Dead Branches, Rocks, and Other "Weapons" of Nature

Even when you are away from home or office, you may have weapons at your disposal. If you are foolish enough to go hiking in the woods without a knife, without a stick, without a flashlight, without a pen, etc., nature provides readymade weapons at your disposal along the trail, and off of it. Below we will just mention the two most obvious.

9.1: Fallen Branches

Fallen branches can be the best defense in the forest, even against wild animals like stray dogs, coyotes, etc. You want to select the longest, lightest, most solid, thickest, and driest branch possible, but not in that order. The solidity is most important, but you have to be able to lift it. You must use common sense.

It shouldn't be too much longer than you are tall, perhaps a little over your head at most. The ideal is probably Japanese Jo staff level, which is about your armpit level, although longer can be good too, like a long staff. The Jo staff is easier to use for the uninitiated than the long staff, in my opinion. You don't want it too brittle, or wet and crumbly. Basically, you want to be able to swing it and not have it break at the first strike. You obviously have to make the best of what you have.

9.2: Rocks

Rocks. Enough said. Rocks can be thrown (fill your pocket with some that will sting the face). Make sure you're a good aim. But rocks don't just have to be thrown. You can grab a rock of the appropriate shape, and employ it in close quarters combat as you would a blunt instrument for striking the hands, belly, neck, face, head, etc.

Conclusion

This was far from an exhaustive look at turning ordinary objects into effective instruments of self-defense. My hope is that it helped broaden your imagination so you will start to see the weapons you have at your disposal wherever you are. As you train with kubotans, knives, staffs, axes, and the like, you will start to notice applications with pens, markers, screwdrivers, rakes, etc.

My advice is to spend some time taking note of possible weapons you have around you in your daily routine—in the kitchen, at the office, in the bedroom, around the yard, on your way to work, in your car, etc. Then, among those options, start thinking about which would be best suited for you personally to use as a defensive instrument if the situation should call for it. This will vary based on your training, or lack thereof, your age, your flexibility, your strength, etc.

Stay safe and always remember that avoidance is your best defense. Screaming, calling the police, and running are your next best defense. Be sure to stay tuned to my website for more to come.

About the Author:

Pat Smith has nearly thirty years' experience in the martial arts. He studied a variety of martial arts styles including Chinese, Japanese, Korean, and American styles.

Pat's broadest experience is in the Chinese styles. He studied a variety of the internal styles of Chinese martial arts that aid health and well-being as well prove to be quite devastating in combat: Chi Kung, Hsing-I Chuan, Pa Kua Chang, and Tai Chi Chuan.

He also studied a number of different Kung Fu styles: Monkey style, various Northern Praying Mantis styles, Northern Shaolin, Sun Pin, and Wing Chun.

His Chinese training included weapons training. In addition, he studied the Chinese grappling arts of Chin-Na and Shuai Jiao.

His experience in the Korean arts includes Tang Soo Do and Tae Kwon Do. The majority of his training in Japanese styles has been in Aikido and Aikijujutsu.

His primary American training is in a rare synthetic Karate style from the Midwest which resembles a combination of Mixed Martial Arts and Israeli Krav Maga, a style tailor made for vicious street self-defense as well as for military and security hand-to-hand combat. Pat has taught Aikijujutsu, Chin-Na, Hsing-I, Kung Fu, the exclusive American synthetic style, and other arts, to select private students. Pat also hosts a martial arts blog, Pat Smith Martial Arts. There is also a Pat Smith Martial Arts Community Page on Facebook. You can follow Pat Smith on Twitter @PatSmithMartial.

Printed in Great Britain
by Amazon